A Beautiful Day In March

By Lucille Washington- Blue   Illustrated by Jamel Carroll

"I am a firm believer in the superpowers of the young mind.

They are like thick sponges ready to seize a world of knowledge".

- **Lucille Washington-Blue**, Author

Dedication

    I would like to dedicate this book to my son, Reginald Blue Jr., and loving grandson (the protagonist) Royal T. Blue.

    Observing how Reggie succeeds in getting his son to maintain a spirit of gratitude through challenging moments - makes me smile.

Acknowledgements from the Author:

In accordance with my book's life lesson, this is my expression of gratitude.

I want to thank the following people for their support:

My very best friend and loving husband - Reginald Blue Sr.; Ms Jenning's Harford Community College creative writing class; Joan Taylor, my cousin and academic supporter; Mary Windhaus, my friend and former neighbor, a retired English instructor from Western High school; Terry Blume, my cousin, a retired teacher; Martha Wallingford, my sister, a Notre Dame honored student; Patricia Carter, my mentor and best friend; Tiffany Washington, my niece and friend; Blondina Bean, my niece and twin on so many levels ;Edith Blume, always a positive inspiration.

Last of all, I want to thank my brother, best friend, and agent: Joseph W. Washington Jr. M.D. - the man who took the title (agent) and ran with it(lol). Without his nagging and persistence, this book would still be forth coming. By the way, Everyone needs an agent like my Jr..

Parental Suggestions

The Author collected a group of words, concepts, and poetic terms you may want to discuss with your child prior to or after reading.

Vocabulary

- P.2: **Protective grasp** - his dad held him safely
- P.4: **Merriment** - happiness, merry/happy Christmas
- P.6: **Crystalline** - like crystals or sparkling glass
- P.9: **Whack** - to hit or strike with force
- P.11: **Uncertainty** - opposite of certain, not sure
- P.16: **Attitude** - the way one choose to feel about someone or something
- P.16: **Gratitude** - to be thankful

- P.16: **Hopscotch** - a child's game in which a player tosses an object into areas of a figure outlined on the ground and hops through the figure and back to regain the object

Literary Terms

Suggested for discussion after the story:

P.8: **Simile** - using (like or as) to make a comparison to something unrelated. For example: "slowly lowered his heels as if he were a balloon stuck by a nail."
What does this simile suggest? Have your child create an example.

P.9: **Alliteration** - Using several words that begin with the same or similar consonants.
Ask what is the letter or words being used? Have your child create an example.

P.11: **A BLESSED Day** - A special day - a gift from God to be thankful for.

Food for thought:

P. 7: Why is Royal shown wearing a crown in the mirror, but not outside the mirror?
P.11: What is the moral to the story, or lesson learned?

Excited! Royal T. Blue woke up, stood on his tiptoes and shouted, "Today is my day. It's my birthday!" He decided this day was too important for house rules. So, he left his comforter where he threw it, on the floor at the foot of the bed. Although, he was taught to walk in the house, today the four-year-old chose to run instead.

His parents laughed as they heard little feet galloping

toward their room. Father quickly hid behind the door, knowing his jolly boy would burst in soon. The instant he entered, Dad grabbed him from behind. Royal gasped! but quickly recognized his father's protective grasp.

He tossed his son into the air and spun him around.
Then Dad made funny faces as he joked and clowned. Startled and tickled, the little fellow laughed with joy, for he knew he was the special birthday boy.

Mom joined the merriment. On her knees, she greeted Royal with a hug and kiss. "Special days like this, your mom would never miss." She then held his shoulders and looked into his eyes. "Now, I'm going to bake you a sweet birthday surprise!"

Royal licked his lips

and said, "Yummy, yummy, I can't wait! Mommy is baking me a strawberry short-cake." The cheerful birthday boy knew his mother would bake his favorite.

In preparations for his day, Dad gave Royal a warm bubble bath with his favorite rubber ducky. Afterwards, he dressed him in a glittering suit. Royal squealed, "Gee! I am Lucky!"

Proudly smiling at his handsome son, he said, "When you wear this suit, there will be no doubt, as to whom this beautiful day is all about."

The black suit was pure silk with an awesome sheen. It was highlighted with shimmering gold, silver, and green. These colors reflected from a crystalline bowtie and jacket button. This made Royal's royalty clear and sudden.

"Wow!" Royal said. In the mirror he saw a prince. Standing on his tiptoes, he sang and danced. "Today is my day. It's my birthday!"

Leaving his bedroom, the young prince did cartwheels across the floor all the way to the front door.

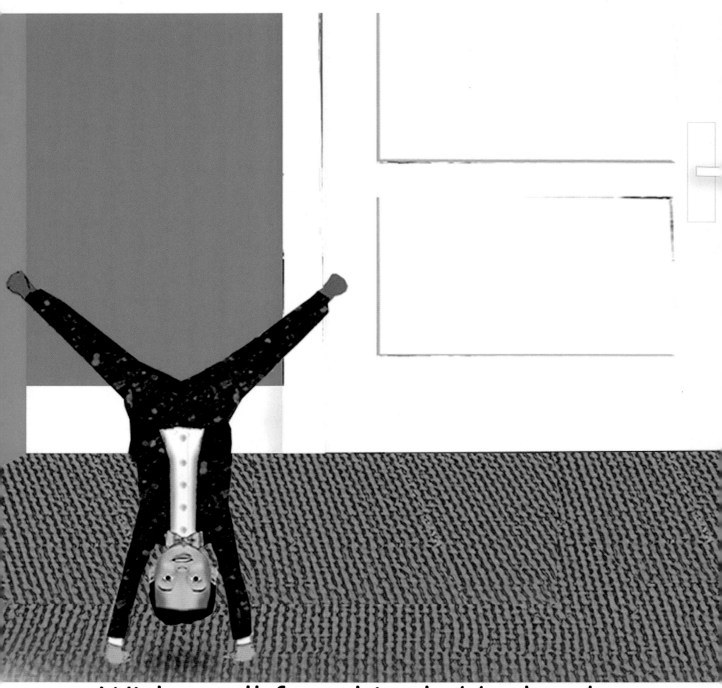

With a pull from his chubby hands, he flung the door open and stood on his tiptoes. Then and all at once ... Royal slowly lowered his heels as if he were a balloon stuck by a nail.

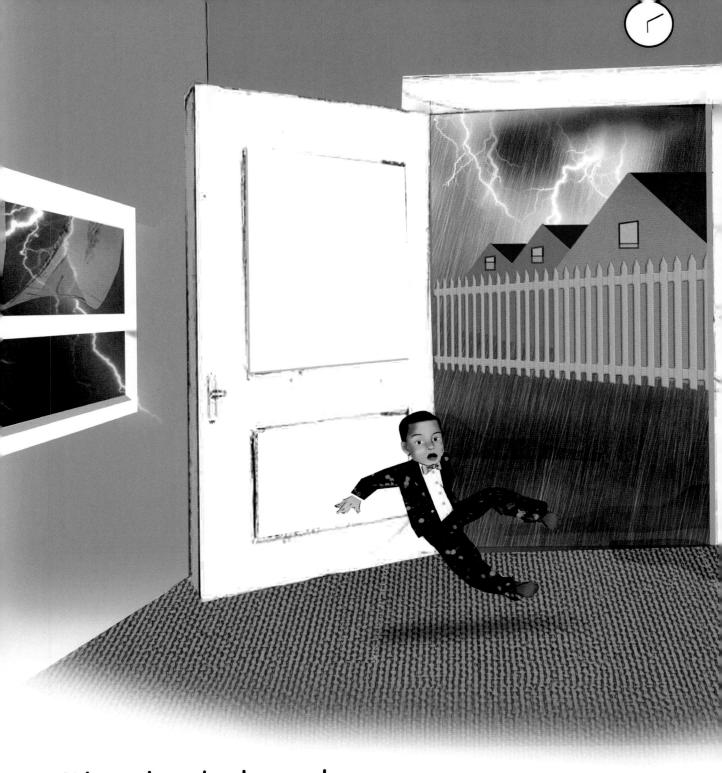

The sky darkened. Powerful rain built puddles. Lightning cracked the sky as thunder roared. Wind whirled through the door, violently whipped the window sheers and whacked the birthday boy to the floor. Then came a second gust that slammed the door shut!

Frightened! Royal leaped to his feet and sprang into his father's opened arms where he sensed a place of safety and calm.

Mr. Blue hugged his son closely.

"It's a beautiful day in March," he assured him. He smiled at his sobbing, royal prince, and chanted - "Today is your day! It's your birthday! Today is y..."   "But Dad!" Little Blue interrupted. He pushed away from his father's chest. Then searched his eyes for answers as he hoped for the best. "Today is a bad day, and no one will come to my birthday party."

"Oh no! said his father.

Even through the storm, you must stay thankful. You see, there is always a reason for each season. In fact, today is a BLESSED day! March winds are blowing the winter away. Rain showers are watering the grass and trees. Creating a beautiful day for your guests to see.

Fighting back tears, the little prince sniffed, and smiled with uncertainty.

Like a click of a switch, the storm silenced! The little prince quickly looked towards the window and witnessed a royal surprise: The sun brightening the sky; The wind at peace; The rain ceased.

Little Boy Blue slipped from his father's grip, and charged to the front door with a flip!

Warm air embraced his plump, smiling face. The sun fully bloomed the cherry blossoms; dried the freshly, greened grass; and again on his tiptoes, the birthday boy sang and danced.

Finally, guests arrived from far and near. Far more guests than Royal could ever dream. They brought gifts wrapped in sparkling paper and glittering bows. He ripped open his presents while dancing on his toes. "Today is my day! It's my birthday!" Royal T. Blue felt like royalty.

Grownups watched as children played outside. Some wanted just to bounce and slide, while others chose to hang-glide. They played his favorite - hide and seek, and jumped rope until it tangled at their feet. Kids played Superman electronic games where the bad guys got beat-up. And danced to hip-hop as the DJ mixed the beats up.

Royal T. Blue had Tons of fun with his guests.
He has been to lots of parties, but to him this was
best. Thinking about the storm, he recalled how his
dad taught him to change his attitude. So on his
knees, Royal gave God a prayer of gratitude:
"Thank you Lord for blowing the winter away,
and allowing my guest to come safely and play."

From hop-scotch to hip-hop and to the strawberry shortcake they scoffed,
it was indeed -

a beautiful day in March.

About the Author:

In 1997, Lucille Washington-Blue received a B.A. degree in marketing from College of Notre Dame, MD. She also took courses in children's literature. As a former Trinity A.M.E. Sunday school superintendent, she wrote her first play, The Lord's Prayer from a Child's Mind.

Lucille retired as a finance clerk from Verizon in 2007. After retiring, she did volunteer work at Harford County Public Library in programs entitled, Sharing the Gift, and Partners in Reading. These programs included tutoring, and reading dramatically to and with children - her passion.

She also wrote a reading curriculum, Bringing Books to Life - a 10 step, experiential learning program. In her community, children call her Aunt Lucy, so she named her community children's book club, Aunt Lucy Bringing Books to Life. Her students read and performed Aunt Lucy's rewritten classics at their community library.

So, it is only fitting that Lucille's first book was written to encourage parent/child interaction, introduce literary concepts, and enrich vocabulary.

In addition, as with everything she does with children, her book - A Beautiful Day in March - teaches a moral lesson: Be grateful for your blessings even through the storm, for it too shall pass.

About the Illustrator

Illustrator, Jamel Carroll, 26, is a senior at Pace University where he majors in Art and recently painted a ground breaking wall mural for the library entrance. He has illustrated four other books entitled: "Jordan and Nelle's Adventure Before Christmas", "Positive Quotes for Little Ones", "To My Child: You Are Perfect" and "Mandy the not so Magnificent Helper".

His passion for art, no doubt, continues to shine through his complementary story telling ability in "A beautiful day in March.

Made in the USA
Monee, IL
20 December 2019

19355415R00017